YOUR KNOWLEDGE HAS VALUE

Fredrik Utesch

Contemporary Sino-Africa Relations

Concerns and opportunities

GRIN Verlag

Bibliografische Information der Deutschen Nationalbibliothek:

Die Deutsche Bibliothek verzeichnet diese Publikation in der Deutschen National-
bibliografie; detaillierte bibliografische Daten sind im Internet über http://dnb.d-
nb.de/ abrufbar.

Imprint:

Copyright © 2013 GRIN Verlag GmbH
Druck und Bindung: Books on Demand GmbH, Norderstedt Germany
ISBN: 978-3-656-49092-0

This book at GRIN:

http://www.grin.com/en/e-book/231976/contemporary-sino-africa-relations

GRIN - Your knowledge has value

Der GRIN Verlag publiziert seit 1998 wissenschaftliche Arbeiten von Studenten, Hochschullehrern und anderen Akademikern als eBook und gedrucktes Buch. Die Verlagswebsite www.grin.com ist die ideale Plattform zur Veröffentlichung von Hausarbeiten, Abschlussarbeiten, wissenschaftlichen Aufsätzen, Dissertationen und Fachbüchern.

Visit us on the internet:

http://www.grin.com/

http://www.facebook.com/grincom

http://www.twitter.com/grin_com

CONTEMPORARY

SINO – AFRICA RELATIONS

Concerns and opportunities

By

Fredrik Utesch

Chinese Diplomacy

School of Social Development and Public Policy

Fudan University

Table of Contents

Introduction

In 1955 the first Afro-Asian Bandung conference was conducted a first step for the development of the Sino-African relationship. Just one year later the first relation between an African country, Egypt, and China was signed. Since then, many new relation agreements were signed. Up to now, there exist 49 relations between African countries and China. With these settlements much development between the African continent and China has occurred. Not only political connections were established, but also support on international levels was given between the countries. Also business sector relations were made, as well as cultural and social exchanges realized. Historical moments were shared and the economies on both sides of the relations rose. During the years a lot of chances for development, especially in supporting the African countries were taken, especially investments from the Chinese side. With this, new opportunities came up and respect from other countries regarding this relationship encouraged; however, concerns are evolving from the African population and westernized countries.

Within this paper, I will first of all reveal the history and development of the relationships between countries of the African continent and China. Further on, I will talk about the opportunities and concerns seen by those nations directly involved and also those seen from a westernized point of view. To sum up the paper, I will highlight prospects and possible future developments between Africa and China.

The development of Sino-Africa relations

The first steps

To understand the contemporary situation and the relationships between African countries and China, it is important to take a look at the development of the relationships and their common history. A common era is 1. October 1949, a time when the People's Republic of China got proclaimed. In the 1950s African countries, including Sudan, Libya, Ghana and Tunisia got independence. Sino – African relations are looking back to a joint history of 57 years. Beginning, May 1956, when China signed its first diplomatic relation in Africa with Egypt. Within 15 years, from 1956 on, China developed diplomatic relations with up to 44 different African countries. During that time, China not only sent health aid directly to African countries but also offered military support via training and weapons to support the independent movement of its African partners.

Reasons for the orientation towards Africa and its implementation

China feels until now obliged to support struggling African countries, due to its own historical background in times of oppression in colonialism. In its African policy, this is one of the major points to support those countries. Furthermore, influence of the West and the Soviet Union in Africa should be diminished and support was sought to counter recognition of Taiwan as the representative at the UN.[i] To achieve this situation China moreover used financial investments and projects to get a good reputation among African countries and support on the topics mentioned earlier. One project for example was the invitation to students from Africa and let them study at Chinese universities – paid by the Chinese government. A major infrastructure project by China from 1970 until 1975 was its built and financed TAZARA resp. TANZAM or also called Uhuru (Swahili – Freedom) railway. With this project, China financed Zambia's economic independence of the South African .The end stations of the railway track are Kapiri Mposhi in Zambia and the port of Tanzania, Dar es Salaam.[ii]

In 1971, Chinas strategy gained profit when it substituted Taiwan as a member and the representative of China in the UN with the help from its African associates. Today, only 5 African countries, Burkina Faso, Swaziland, Malawi, The Gambia, Sao Tome and Principe, do not support China regarding the "One China Policy". This means, that these countries don't see Taiwan as a part of The People's Republic of China. Furthermore, they have the opinion, that the Republic of China is the one and only representative of China. On the one hand, after this strategic success for China, political support was to this time not anymore a main requirement and furthermore the African countries couldn't provide the expertise and technology needed. But also, because on the other hand, China lost its good reputation during the civil war in Angola by taking the site of the United States. Years of downswing within the Sino-Africa relation was the result. However, in 1989 the value of African partnerships rose again. The cause of improved relations with Africa was not only the repeated loss of China's support from the West due to the Tiananmen Square Protest in Beijing, but also because the Soviet Union broke up. Albeit, China could now trust its African partners on an international level. The concentration of western countries on Africa abated with the end of the Cold War in 1991.

The "five points proposal", "FOCAC" and "the year of Africa"

The President during this time, Jiang Zemin, saw the opportunity for China and offered 1996 a "Five Points Proposal" to African countries to strengthen and structure the relationships.[iii] Following, in year 2000 the "FOCAC – Forum of China-Africa Cooperation" was established. During the next years, the partnerships and trades between Africa and China developed exponentially.

The year 2006 was officially named as the year of Africa by the PRC. Not only a FOCAC, with 48 African countries participating took part in Beijing, but also a "white paper" got published by Chinese government. This states a milestone in Sino-Africa relations. The white paper includes eight measures concerning the strategic cooperation between the People's Republic of China and its African partners, as well as a new orientation China's towards Africa. Furthermore, with this paper, the Chinese government pointed out that it is not interested in a short, superficial relationship with African countries, but interested in long term bilateral connections.[iv]

Following the FOCAC and the publicity of the white paper, investments of US$ 9billion on the African continent where signed in 2006.[v] Furthermore, developing aid for the African partner countries was set during the Africa tour of Wen Jiabao. For instance, schools and hospitals should be built. Political connections strengthened and several leaders of the high levels visited each other.

Contemporary situation

Nowadays, between 750,000 and one million Chinese people work and or live in Africa and approximately 700 and 900 Chinese companies currently do business in almost every country in Africa. Most of the Chinese companies doing business in Africa are State-Owned-Companies or belong in some way to the government; only some are private-owned. During the last years, however, the government tried to motivate more private-owned companies to do business in and with Africa. 49[vi] (2007) African countries hold diplomatic relations with China today. As a result, between 2009 and 2012 China not only got the leading trading partner but also the main creditor and the second largest donor and third largest investor on the African continent. In 2011, the Sino-Africa bilateral trade value hit the $ 166billion line and grew between 2000 and 2011by US$ 150billion[vii] Investments from China are rising and Tourists from China are going on vacation and safaris to African countries. Relations on the economic and political but also cultural and social aspect are getting deeper and exchanges between political and leaders but also within the population, for instance within students, is increasing.

To summarize the development of almost six decades of Sino-Africa relations from the 1950's until today, it can be said that the progress between African countries and China took major steps. Until now, these relations stay under a good mood seen from both sides. Although, China is a far more developed developing country compared to its counterparts in Africa, respect and no political interference is an important point for both sides. Special-Economic-Zones were established and the bilateral trade grew disproportionately. China supported the African partner countries with financial and educational aid, extended its foreign direct investments and trade cooperation's. Africa on the other hand, supported China on international questions (e.g. 1971, when they voted for China to get his place as a member in the UN).

Opportunities and Concerns

Through the process of globalization and worldwide competition, not only African countries became dependent on China's support, but also vice versa. Without Africa's resources, China's manufactories couldn't produce for a very long time. In a lot of subdivisions within natural resources the PRC is leading in the area of consumption. China's sources on the local resource market do not cover the existing demand. It has to analyze the worldwide market with its opportunities and Africa with its enormous amount of resources. A lot of resources in Africa are not exploited yet and a massive potential is still available. Albeit, China is not the first visitor in the African market looking for business opportunities in the division of natural resources. Western companies have already been there for a long time and China has to wait and analyze the possible opportunities emerging.

Comparing to western companies, China is following a different strategy in the African market to become business partners for new projects. Political situations and the form of government in target countries play a different role. Where China sticks to its rule not to interfere in political situations and no strings attached, westernized companies do not or even cannot operate in that way. For China and its companies, this is a huge opportunity to get contracts in countries where a large occurrence of resources are available. The strategy of "no strings attached" and "no interference" is also nowadays often a game changer for decisions made by the African government. Africa's government wants to develop themselves without any interference of regulations regarding deals with other nations and their companies. This is also illustrated through the historical background of colonialism.
As a conclusion it can be said that for African governments the FDI's of China, are attractive business offers and Chinese foreign policy is a crucial element of the Sino-African relationship nowadays.

Furthermore, China is not only looking for the resources on the African country to satisfy its demand but also for investment opportunities with a bride future. Chinese companies especially focused in the past on hydropower and infrastructure projects and also plan to extent those investments. In these fields they still see a huge potential and high priority to other fields of investment. Albeit, China is not the only

"BRIC" country who does its business in Africa and sees opportunities for the future. India is already China's biggest competitor regarding to the volume of trade in Africa and India's Prime Minister Manmohan Singh just announced a new era for the Indian-Africa relation in Africa. In 2015, the trade volume shall cross the US$ 90 billion line.

Bilateral trade volume 2012	
China	US$ 198.5 billion[viii]
Indien	US$ 33.0 billion[ix]

Why does the Chinese government and the Chinese companies see infrastructure as key investments in African countries?

The economy in Africa suffers also because roads are not in a good condition. It takes much more time to deliver products from the place of resource exploitation to a harbor for instance. Additionally, costs are getting higher for reparation on the trucks and through the time lost because of bad road conditions. An already fulfilled supreme example is the TANZAM railway built, planned and financed by Chinese companies. Some more railway projects, which were all signed by Chinese companies in Africa in 2012, are for example modernizations of railway systems in Djibouti, Nigeria and Ethiopia as well as sales of locomotives to South Africa; it is worth $3.4 billion.[x] So, to boost the economy of Africa and make it more interesting for foreign and also for local investors, it is important to first build the infrastructure and then go on with further steps. If step one is not done, the following steps will suffer or even not be possible to fulfill. Through better infrastructure, companies, investments and the complete economy will grow. As a conclusion more energy is needed and another sector with large future opportunities accrues. If the energy sector is not growing simultaneously to the growth rate of the country of faster the energy system of the country will collapse, as seen in India the last years.

However, with development new problems emerge and with fast development as processed within the Sino-Africa relations, those problems will not be less. Additionally, westernized news media upset people with "bad stories" about China's allegedly worse strategy in Africa during the last years. African people and even some governments got influenced by those and change their mind about China as a partner. A term, called "China Threat" emerged on the African continent. As Chinese companies experienced, problems regarding language and culture are a big topic to take care of. In which language for example shall Chinese communicate with Africans or what is the culture of the people? A lot of Chinese companies brought vast or even all of their employees from China at the beginning. So, communication problems didn't come up in first place within the company. Albeit, with rising investments in Africa it became a perceptible problem.

Firstly, complaints about non-employment of local people by Chinese companies in Africa is increasing within the African population and industry. Furthermore, it is also not always possible for Chinese companies to bring the workers from China. As a conclusion, African people got employed more than before. On the one hand, the lack of education is seen, but on the other hand, more professional trainings should be offered to improve this lack. This step is already taking part, but it still has to be improved. China brings knowledge and also experience to Africa, the local companies and people can profit from this, if co-operations are made and trainings offered. But to do so, company and political leaders have to be on the same side and should support each other and exchange the individual experiences. But most of the Chinese companies in Africa are SOE's and competitors to the local companies. If it is already hard for well experienced private Chinese companies to compete against the state-owned-companies in Africa, how shall it be possible for local ones, who don't have that experience? [xi].

Another concern, which came up from the African side during the last years is that some Chinese companies don't stick to the diverse national laws. The Chinese government perceived this problem as well, albeit it hard to control all of the companies acting in Africa from the side of Chinese government. A lot of small and medium-sized companies doing their business in Africa and who don't stick to the rules set regarding environmental protection, work safety or employment law for instance. Those concerns and more problems, awake criticism within the African population and now also within the politician. Lamido Sanusi, president of Nigeria's central bank, said that China was contributing to Africa's "de-industrialization and underdevelopment." [xii] He further more said, "That was also the essence of colonialism..."[xiii]

A discord between some Chinese Companies and a growing number of African populations is growing and the governments of the African countries who sign contracts with Chinese companies for projects should not look away. Instead they should think about a good way to profit from the Chinese investments and companies in the country and on the other hand protect the local companies.

An occurring problem regarding this decision making process is that though due to the hardly-transparency systems of giving aid to Africa by China, it is not easy to allocate where the money is really going and politicians put a part of the money in the own pocket.

For African countries, China is a very different partner then countries from the EU or for instance the United States. Regulations regarding taking a credit or loan are totally different and it is more convenient. Where partnerships with western countries often are connected to regulations regarding the human rights development and political development, China sticks to his African policy of "no interference" and "no strings attached". Chinese companies focus on the business and its opportunity. With focus of getting needed financial help there are big differences comparing the western countries and China. In China's way of thinking, the investor does not need to check if a country or company can allow oneself the credit given. Regarding to the African countries, it is the responsibility of each African government who wants to make use of a credit. From the Chinese point of view, the responsible, if a country will profit from a deal with another country is its government itself and not the country doing business with. It is not China's duty, that the African countries don't have an overall China strategy. China wants to make business with each country separately and doesn't see Africa as a big country with 54 provinces. So, for African countries it is more convenient to lend the money needed for projects etc. from China instead of sticking to some additional regulations, given by other investing countries.

Furthermore, some economists from South Africa said, that Africa should think about a way to improve regarding the unequal trade balance to China. African counterparts to China should also set a focus on the manufacturing and not only on the exploitation and directly selling. African countries could get a larger amount of the value chain, which would support the employment rate and also the trade balance.[xiv] The African countries could profit more from the Sino-African relations.

Conclusion and prospects

Due, to this large and fast development, which took part through the almost last 6 decades, new opportunities and chances have emerged. New business fields got developed and new relations between Sino-Africa were signed. Both economies grew during these days of partnership, although in their different ways and strength. It is conspicuous that both profit in their different ways from this relation. China on the one hand gets its needed resources ("Oil and coal accounted for 50 percent of China's imports from Africa in 2012[xv])

Whereby Africa gets its needed financial support. Furthermore, to a greater extent exchanges developed between African countries and their partner China in fields of politics, economics, cultures and social. Exchanges of youths and scholars for students emerged. Built on this basis, positive prospects in the future exist. With the following bilateral prospects of the Sino-Africa relations, I would like to highlight the possible future developments and complete this paper.

As already on large going, but still a huge space of improvement existing is in the bilateral trade sector. China could profit much more from the diversity provided by the product range of African countries. Africa's food sector offers a lot of diverse game products, which are exotics on the other countries. Through to Chinas enormous economical up movement, the population demanding fancy and diverse food is increasing. Moreover, Africa's landscapes and diversity of its fauna offer a large sector for tourism. Many African countries have already established this market years or decades ago albeit, tours offered by Chinese travel agencies is still less with potential. Another chance exists through the large and young population in Africa and the current development of the countries. A shift in the existing class of buyers is already taking part and the change can be expected in a greater extent within the next decade. Thus, new field of business opportunities will emerge and field for investments will grow. For this step, which China already experienced within the last decades, the knowledge of people with that experienced is needed. A field of new business opportunity for Chinas service industry is developing.

Moreover, a think tank between westernized countries and China regarding aid for Africa should be established. So experienced can be exchanged and the ways of giving aid effectively can get improved. For me, the current Sino-Africa relations show a huge potential of bilateral support in developing their economies with large and diverse opportunities in the future.

References

[i] Li Anshan, Robert I. Rotberg (Editor), "China's New Policy toward Africa", China into Africa: Trade, Aid and Influence, 2008

[ii] He Wenping, Partners in Development, Beijing Review, No. 44 Nov. 2, 2006

[iii] http://www.fmprc.gov.cn/eng/ziliao/3602/3604/t18035.htm

[iv] Li Anshan, China and Africa: Policy and Challenges, China Security, Vol.3, No.3, p. 69-93, 2007

[v] Foster, Butterfield, Chen, Pushak, Building Bridges: China's Growing Role as Infrastructure Financier for Sub-Saharan Africa, 2009

[vi] Alden, Chris, China in Africa, Zed Books 14, 2007

[vii] Ron MacIntosh, Chris Roberts, Conference Summary Record – China and Canada in Africa: Interests, Strategies and African Perspectives, 2012

[viii] http://www.scmp.com/news/china/article/1231786/african-companies-fear-chinas-corporate-invasion

[ix] http://www.dw.de/china-india-court-africa-for-resources/a-16699676

[x] http://www.un.org/africarenewal/magazine/january-2013/china-heart-africa

[xi] http://www.scmp.com/news/china/article/1231786/african-companies-fear-chinas-corporate-invasion

[xii] http://www.scmp.com/news/china/article/1231786/african-companies-fear-chinas-corporate-invasion

[xiii] http://www.scmp.com/news/china/article/1231786/african-companies-fear-chinas-corporate-invasion

[xiv] http://www.dw.de/china-india-court-africa-for-resources/a-16699676

[xv] http://www.upi.com/Business_News/Energy-Resources/2013/03/27/China-tightens-grip-on-Africas-resources/UPI-76001364420752/